Praise for *Chalk Song*

This is a brilliant collaboration, wherein these poets' voices cross-pollinate, converge, and diverge to bring us sensibilities that accommodate the strangeness of Chauvet Cave. With each poem, Batchelder, Berger-Jones, and Evans take us deeper and deeper into the cave, while challenging our efforts to understand what Herzog calls "the first evidence of the modern human soul." Just as these poets take us deeper into the world of the cave—the horse paintings, the bear skulls, the hand with the crooked finger—they just as easily give us passage out of that world, with unexpected, breathtaking imagery: "a new moon's Motown," a "flickering projectionist," "the mandrake genome," taking us deeper and deeper into unknowability.

–Duy Doan, author of *We Play a Game*

"Our hieroglyphs are loose," say the caverns of this magical book. Yes, they are. These poets take language to the frontiers of intelligibility, and then hold it there, right where you want it. Drop with them into Grotte Chauvet-Pont d'Arc. Lock eyes with, and bring again to mind, paintings brought out of minds we once had (and somehow still must have), when, some 32,000 years ago, as Frost would say, nature exceeded itself in us, and what had only been formed began to make form: cave-lions on and within walls, on Herzog's screens, and now both on and within these pages. Spelunkers, climb in.

–Mark Richardson, editor of *The Letters of Robert Frost*

CHALK SONG

A Collaboration
Gale Batchelder
Susan Berger-Jones
Judson Evans

LILY POETRY REVIEW BOOKS

To our animal bodies all things have the capacity for speech—
although very few things speak in words. For any movement
may be felt as a gesture, and any sound may be heard as a voice
laden with expressive or communicative intent.

The Spell of the Sensuous, David Abram

Throughout the cave there is, strikingly, little foreground
present, no line of landscape or vegetation on which these
creatures exist. They have no habitat save the rock and the
dark, and as such they seem to float free, unmoored from the
world. These animals live, as Simon McBurney memorably puts
it, "in an enormous present, which also contained past and
future. A present in which nature was not only contiguous
with them, but continuous. They flowed in and out of a
continuum of everything around them; just as the animals flow
into and out of the rock. And if the rock was alive, so were the
animals. Everything was alive."

Underland: A Deep Time Journey, Robert Macfarlane

Will we ever be able to understand the vision of the artist over
such an abyss of time?

The Cave of Forgotten Dreams, Werner Herzog

Published by Lily Poetry Review Books
223 Winter Street
Whitman, MA 02382

https://lilypoetryreview.blog/

ISBN: 978-1-7375043-0-6

Design: Martha McCollough

Cover photo: Claude Valette   *(licensed under under the Creative Commons Attri-bution-Share Alike 4.0 International license)*

Comment on Collaboration

Werner Herzog's *Cave of Forgotten Dreams*, which inspired our experiment in collaboration, traces multiple approaches to the provocative
otherness of stunning Paleolithic cave art. Various scientists use
laser technology to map the negative space of the cave complex.
Paleontologists compare the works to other figurative traditions,
while the "sniffer"—a perfumer—searches for undiscovered caves
by using his olfactory sense to sniff out the distinct underground air
emanating from a cave.

With *Chalk Song,* the three of us challenged each other to use as many
imaginative and linguistic resources as we could muster to come at the
generative unknowability of these works of art and their world. Our
poems were engendered in evolving response to the worlds of the cave
and Herzog's film, which changed shape in all our imaginations as we
traded readings, images, and ideas from our ongoing research.

Equally, each poem was shaped by the sense that it was entering a
region already conditioned by the poetic choices made by the others;
it became another particle between two already charged particles.
Because we read and commented on, often at length, each other's
drafts, a certain permeability and cross-pollination resulted, borrowed
gestures or vocabulary. Sometimes a line that originated in one writer's
poem was edited out and later appeared in another permutation in a
collaborator's poem.

We were never really tempted to blur our separate voices into one
voice, despite an experiment in writing a collective poem, which
did not get into the manuscript. Our approach was guided by
Robert Creeley's collaborations with visual artists, of which he said
"if collaboration is to be at all successful, it must be the result of
different individuals…working together to make something that is
larger than any one sensibility."

Contents

Three: Buried Constellation

VOICE PRINTS

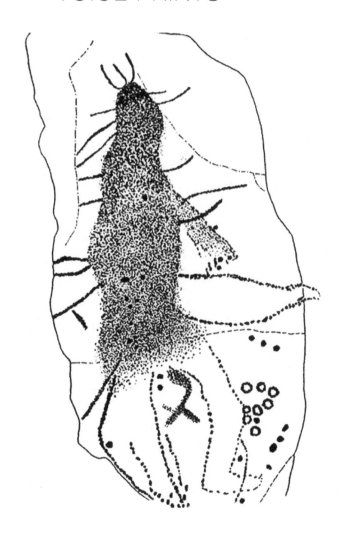

Chauvet-Pont-d'Arc

I am dark and near dying

I want you to tell only the light in my fur,
bright as fire

Cut as with teeth in char and blood
spooning shapes, a defile between hills,
side by side on both or all feet at once
in steps that cannot be mistaken
across the crumble of sheaves

Red palm alone with crooked finger
an abrupt shiny echo, the color of snow

Mind in the Cave

If I've pulled free   I still find the shadow
on your side of the bed.

You were the preventable
accident   shaman at the core of sediments

flickering projectionist   when you sang
there was no room in the world   but listening.

Voice-over stanches   the nick and smear
where we'd kneel in the mud when glass curtain walls
were gone   press votives of clay and quartz
into fissures   live images congealed.

Clicking your tongue   counting rhyme
for the myth there ever was
an outside.

You'd forgotten the way out   chambers folded back in the score
to see what you might unleash from me   Swiss Army knife
panicked   open.

Just as the eye was reinvented many times   first as brittle star –
we would see through our skin   and couldn't sleep
so much seeping into us   as we broke   into islands

Where do our fingers end   and flames begin?

You taught me how the world   retracts
to a city of words   scuffed
to rubble with your heel.

Time-depths   several fresh starts   burials
and exhumations below touch   or reach or
accusation.

You offered a hand
from the other side of death   its seal of red impact
its crooked thumb.

Paper Sky

Ink wounds the sky
          full of swallows
                    filling the weather with dusk

*

Our cities are also surrounded by revolution's fur
          as the weather is mobbed by our elbows

*

Of chiaroscuro and aqua-print in this furry place

*

Nothing to do but sit like handprints
          to listen to our flowers in flight

*

Noting the daffodils and sunsets
          where the people sleep

*

As if one could draw them
          as slim as rainbows
        in this slight palace, blued by winter's dust

*

We all feel too vulnerable dressed only in blue crayon

*

From arias to nudes, scalloped, nightlong

Untitled (Chauvet 2)

The little song hardly begun,
you asked whether anything
falling inward flashed in the ice.

High on a rock you listened,
parched air rushing sleek
and agile into the chamber,
the swirl of storm-eye snapping
even the narrowest gleam
of twin near planets. Bones
of its passing choked the usual
thousand responses, in its wake
the low hum of padded soles
like brushes across drum skin.

Little (Subterranean) Song

Here is where atlas makes room for x-ray. Shepherd stone shatters
cuneiform. If cameras perch long enough for ice ledges
to melt, the turnstiles will be ready
for their handprints. The conundrum tail catches
in its windpipe.

Throw your voice as you would an opponent contending
a crawlspace. And your voice finds its way through
the fissure. Only your voice without parent or protector.

Your poor orphan voice leaves its score on the rock.

Combed Horses

Up to the edge of flotsam
                    (we are)

ledge refrained
cloud gossip
a scribbled dandruff
weather's orphanage –

what may be said
to define the snow
from our secrets?

Earth meets its margins
then larks a way
through a night's turnstiles –

a bruised hum
                    (we are)

an atlas for
          a thousand private brushes –

our hieroglyphs are loose.

Sun Made Blue

If dusk could talk / water walk / all red then
We wear white undone / all our shoes, mud
Sand in our tunes / organ water pipes
Sprinting into the news / hand over foot-tumble
So many secrets / the holy ones / seeping through sheer
We giant across the land / green hours

Open the shutters / close the shutters
No one / watching the backs / marked X
As though we could walk a hand / outstretched
The race of sepia against stone / wheels up
Our hair aflame and our skin / chalked

Communicating Vessels

I learn by being listened for, see
by being sought. Your face stirs
the underground wind of *there/not there*

I can breathe harder or softer, but I am broomflower,
I disappear up close up,
grafted to distance.

My skull's pit organ
of heat-seeking doesn't need to touch
to take samples

or umbels deeper down, stung honey
and amber, sinuses beyond five finger's sense,
unstopped by anything held still

as you kneel to press thighs
and crotch into my contour, learn
my difficult dead language.

A wind might focus a song through me,
but I will never sing one. I'll never blow that bubble –
no need for another world

since I can cross the breath-on-window closeness
to occur like a whim from the throb
of one rickshaw vein.

Keep your hand exactly *there* and *there*
that's what these silences,
these blank pages are for –

All my openings are the texture
of a glove pulled inside
-out, epoxy and asbestos of milkweed fiber.

By the time you close your eyes to sort
through all my particles
I've gathered you from all angles.

I already have enough of you.

Combed Horses

What may be said
if we break
our colloquial winds

             into violets

like trade pillows
          (here)
or the baffled dawn

           under
               (no, inside)
          celadon dust

with lard & vent pole
telegraphs have contrail fur

          & gravity must be bare
          a shagged O
          for glottal secretion
          beside dazzling rag fire
          where we forget
               (we are)

yellow, uninvited & world-like –

who would put a dandelion here?

Here Dreams a Curve of Cave Wall

      (We are)
here to test
fleck of skin rubbed
white as if washed by licking,

ledges stained in scent
of gore-wound, child's

rough footprints soothed
by falling dust and charcoal,

the little hand placed through
to still the chorus of chalk hooves.

      (You are)
undercurrent ribs and musk
lodestar in windpipe time
thrown air
an offering bowl.

Stringed Somehow

The jars are on fire

Somewhere the night has flown

Names no longer come in choruses

We are girdles for June

Our hands are dust sisters

Somehow still in arms

As furious beams or mighty hues

Never heard of again inside burrows

We walk down streams like dawn misters

We blow away a thousand drawn swans

Sometimes blurbs line our lint barracks

To draw dusk with paw-print rain

Bird Brain

There are many here who want to talk
to clouds of pollen or stale dust waiting
for a finger. Asterisks of mobbing
birds on the monitor.

In hawk feathers, you are opposite of Orpheus,
dismissing fear with a watershed of kills.

You open body's empty purse, climb
inside to costume yourself
in lookout and camouflage.

Pray to the sanctity of lodestars, stopgaps.
Deep rave of limbers damped beneath the blind.

You work loose the necklace, unlacing vein
or tendon, chokers and chains from the drawer
of bloody jewels. You stencil
slack bellies of young white flourish.

There are many here who date themselves by
rings of decay, ratio of trace elements to trance
states, who are left learning
the alphabet through open wounds.

My Tattoo Parlor

By the end of the Iron Age I was gliding off the tundra, bouncing from
my sugary after-birth. I thought that the belly of my Mother
had held me, but no, she had simply stenciled me into her underpants.

Her wounds made many cuneiform rounds after I was born so
I was gentle with her. I drew blue skies over her storms. I hopped
in & out of her song. One day she ate winter & then drank the sea.

I asked the sea: Will my heart clog the inside of a cockleshell?
Will I learn how to eat without mauling sunlight?
Am I made of bird-gas, airy & fresh?

The more I threw the sky into my eyes, the more the earth blued.
The more I hummed to blue, the more raindrops shattered. Stars fell
to each side of the pond, as if light was icing for our universe.

I fluttered away, past currents & ferns, under sudden downpours
flooded with fur. Soft jewels soaked in the shades.
It was blueberry season.

I laugh now as the sky still spreads long, tangled with crows
& summer's sediment. Bare leaves loop through base elements
in a mess of mouse-dew. I dress in moo-moos of endless clover.

Pentimento

You hid skeletal vapor, stringed and blue. Exhale,
a flailing stroke catching gusts flung upward,

lamp made cold, your dust an entreaty held
close. What if caulked what if lost what if no

curve of flank, shade or scrape, rumbled passage
of foot and hoof. There once was a star it burned

in your hand there was no marking no calling
forth, the jagged lines only your eyes half told.

Codex Collapse Syndrome

We sandbag the ventricle leak of ancient light
to restore haloes to the right objects – freezers,
turn signals, microwaves.

Everything is early, spry with milt, the delicate climate
of arrival, draughts of air so narrow our ears fold back
their sounds. Comb over psalms smelt muzzles
from the overlap of horse heads. Music can't
caress itself by these long-playing lassoes.

Contour before line, overtones before the molten bell
of an opening. We are sphinx-cubs in our hiding places.
The sky on our skin still unhewn,
our scribbled brochures of lightning.

Without provisions, a more vulnerable hibernation,
a species liable to the same bad dreams. Then thrash
and release, the fan of landlocked arms. Quick
lime sparks each loaded
cloud or brush.

Anyone can draw a blue bead
on the G.P.S. – forking river for the vector
home, or carve a new nipple
for the salt lick continent.

Was

a river from above   cliff falling   in white and scrub
you forage filament   in a backlit crowd   of rounded
limbs   severed as though torn   by bombs   an embrace
a gouge between legs   while the giant   gesticulates
over the plexiglass box   you want to flee   on animated
flicker   now the white-gloved butler   offers the pale
wooden coffin   for a bone flute   its spine scored
across the axis   as though force of song   could hold
a body erect

watching   eyes rolled back   sockets bright as overflow
always you   the guardian   lampblack marred   and cleft
a basket of horns   press of cheek to neck   tooth to flank
your jaw slack   there will be   a helmet   like a bear skull
to protect   your instruments

Sun Dial Moraine

Not like putting the tongue
to a block of ice, though sharing the numbness
of too many weather-shapes (larger enumerations,
denominations) so nearly full (broader and broader
loops) (I would rather evaporate) of carnivorous
time or coiled crane music (my ear one more chamber, one more
resonator) there is nothing else
to do (the grist drilled from a tombstone's
numbers) unless tapioca folds of
trestle (this fortune cookie
sentence with its fortune tugged
out) could cauterize a rainbow
where (I put my ear
to the chamber wall) long in the face,
the gazelle's first signal (prey to
its predator) is mutation
on the most ingrown arch,
harps on a waving hand, winnowing
dots in a city (palace of leaf mold)
of war before the first
shield finds its weapon

Residual Sonnet

So many turn signals, drowned in avenue puddles,
everything has its leaf mattress,
milt road –

My ways through your worn rain
turn me towards clatter sunk invisibilities
where I am wet among brushed umbrellas –

Draughts of hair and sheets of paper marrow,
musak river and refrigerator slum,
the haunt becomes the winnowing silo our thoughts might steal –

Which takes away my radio heart where I am lost, to a whole species,
as if my sighs could lasso the world
with its cloud dots –

When I listen to you,
I place an ear to your unbearable mold.

BOW

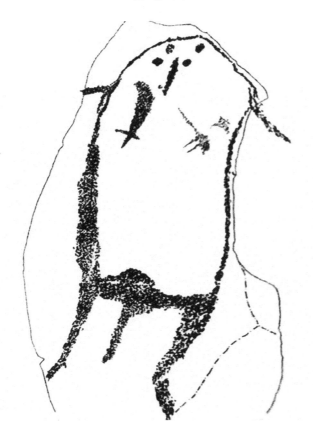

Confetti Score

If your hands had drawn me, would I have been marooned?
Apple polygrams shuck the sky.

Silence paints Dodo birds.
Glistening windows fall asleep in everything I say.

There are miles of twigs and my barley heart withers.
I am a charcoal buffalo, captured in lupine.

Someone sneezes. Daisies flow.
My heather is cloned.

Then I see glyph structures: Us on the Internet.
We are inside our radios, singing beside used molecule lots,

sky-washed among the lilac barnacles of thistle-torn photos.
Now: ravaging the dew.

Carbon dating cannot determine how we walked or slept here
as we dangle from the computer strings of elms.

Who are we? Ektachrome? Cyanotype? Sun Print?
Do we salsify an overbalance to process our committee's buttercups?

Ovals shimmy our laughter into field song.
We hum to dark-sky scales, at home with our fellows,

yet overdrawn to the ends of the Earth.
Will we too be meadows, at the zero hour?

Midnight thoughts bomb the pollen dark.
Our children are heirs to nightshade.

I oxygenate all the O-s in Oxygen.

Noise of Targets

I am hushed voice, as if
puffed-out sprigs of hair
and breath, white foot-candle
on every bevel, stars drawn back
and walkway latticed tight

would incise jaw bones
irradiated pale, drown ocher nostrils,
press ash into stammers.

We're turning up the volume.

Wolf / Boy

Between one footprint and another –
10,000 years.   Balky quiet of one whisper
against the match-struck others, the hard-liners
of breath.   Between one grave
and another in bristlecone time

                         travel, culminations
in history of dance between one moth-blown seed
and briars born on rain,

                         swapped keys of detonation,
crow and fire bicker, commerce out of

                         contour between frame x and $x+1$,
the next, the erasure of integument – the fatty inside

                         of the moment, its put downs
and settlings-in distilled in charcoal against

                         the death drive of rushed red arrow.

Venus on the Rocks

This sky is an earthly measure
dangling from my bracelets.

I am trying to hue holes with bat guano
to create a man from crooked lips.

Would you believe me if I was a hunch-
back under this 3,000 foot ceiling?

Now I am a bird,
mumbling in the clouds.

Would you shoot my human marrow
into pond dents

if I said, "the sky is so inebriated!"
The smaller ones need alibis for their gravy

which is proof that my rib cage
needs a living room for its navel.

When I stand at the edge of
your digs, beware:

history will cry out,
in blindingly high tenses.

Shaded to Half-Life

I used to be a circus man and then
I became an archeologist. I went
into the cave for five days, every night
I was inhabiting lions, because I am
a scientist but a human, too.
            I was not afraid.

Searching for emanations from the interior,
scent of burnt wood and resins, exhalation
of rotting roots twined into limestone above –
this is my personal technique because
            I design perfumes.

Now I can follow the man who made a trail
of handprints, I recognize him by his crooked
little finger, with torch glow he strobe-
danced his own shadow onto the paintings.
            He was six feet tall.

I hear the clackclack of rhino horn against
horn, follow a bison running to escape
this alcove. The lioness in nest of overhang
spurns the advances of her mate – I can see
her curling her lip.
            She is not ready.

I will try to show you how to kill a horse.
Bone point on a wooden shaft a weapon
thrown not only by hand, feathers
to give the spear a good direction. So
it's pretty strong, it's very aggressive.
You can see it would be very difficult for me
            to kill a horse with such a shot.

(Bow)

As play is pronounced pleasure or
　　　　predation   butcher paper kite of laughter
　　　　　　our organs   from the tuning fork of
　　　　　　spine to balsa clef of shoulders
　　　　　　　　practicing the attack fingers on the gut
　　　　　　　as *bow* is Stradivarius and sling blade the
　　　　　　　　concert   hunting band   or four hand rapture
　　　　　　　　remains the afterimage of waste or
　　　　　　　fossil and you embrace the wall
　　　　　　　where you were drawn out
　　　　　　　　　all the athletics of coming to rest
　　　　　　　　　putting yourself on
　　　　　　　　　for so long
　　　　　　　　　　brace against the nothing
　　　　　　　　　　your body had　　become
　　　　　　　　　　　its own lever   taut sinew　　as cast
　　　　　　　　　　　is propulsion and frozen
　　　　　　　　　　　torque　　all the various rafts of the medusa
　　　　　　　　　　you taught me   static
　　　　　　　　　　sends outlets haywire   sapping
　　　　　　　　　our strength before we had to multiply
　　　　　　　　the grindstone world   whittle one upright stem
　　　　　　against another
　　　　　how many parts
　　　are there?
How can one flesh
　　unhand iself
　　arc from the heartwood with taut
　　string theory or find its
　　fingering nock to nipple
the thinking body turning　　turned
to stone

Field Entry (By Fire)

— of space rather than radiant, movement

— flicker, while variations of its second growth

— 10mm of suggested responsivity, so

— smeared apparent, under the angle

— of thickness to startle

— often ox

— one species after another's

— 5 vapors, 2 from undiscovered

— the obstetrical calendar, lilt

— to and fro, as a tall spectrum

— now boxed, snow

— radius to equivalencies, surface

— progenitor: incidental beyond musk

— missing from a geological blue

— silent watercolor per wavelength

— tents, sky

First Day

You polish a thousand umber windows wet-transfer of ink tails
and horse-bramble you call broken blue eyes steel-hurt in places
like harbor land-bridge or car door you have flown by handwritten
pages telling us the lanky one rimmed in rust messages whole
choruses when acrid scent of trapped air becomes camera and light
heft will uncurl shoulders unbuckle the experiment collecting land
mass and snow melt we carry scuff and hum.

Enchanted Entropy

No way to get out of the shot   appendages
in every glimpse
the part that was mostly dragonfly
becomes more collectible with each
obstruction   cross veining and vamping   as they place stones
with such fortitude   at each time-depth   unmovable ever after
though they never stage their shadows   as part of the landscape
or enumerate smeared torch marks
of river music   under the bow of the arch   with 5,000 years
between each page
of sheet music   poor in the form
of happiness   with exhaustive repercussions
digging up graves every time   someone needs
to laugh   which is what the bunched wires
of sight lines excreted by the laser scanner
teach us   the red dots aren't counting off
days like candles under a shot glass   at all
but brightness of the river   or the lute
of snagged grasses   breeding in captivity   just
as there are those who can regenerate
a severed head   and those who can't   based
on how undifferentiated
stem cells of their dreams are

Field Entry (By Flock)

2 rain flowers for radiocarbon
3 quiet grains among yellow silts

30 foldout ore pits
9 left-handed horizons

a tiddlywink fawn
the Fahrenheit scale in streams

10 yeast weeps
1,240 watercolor wars

18 tessellated lily pads
the broken sips of pond-lust

two tiny and used birds
13 dark and parent grasshoppers

one signed butterfly

a sea of punk auroras
a new moon's Motown

6 belly-button roses
11 clouds in girlie Zen

17 credit-sour boy-toy-sarongs
a finger hole for teenage space clunk

a jar of elastic graze
a box dented for planetary zest

40 solid-state mini-squirts
the final minuets of peeps

8 chewy false tarts
1 molten etch-a-scorch

A pinch of cupidinous tinsel moon

Last Day of the Experiment

How I learned to hieroglyph listening
to cave walls, intervals on the treble scale

an epidemic scatter, stammering uphill. I never
wanted roar of red, falsified sins, six hundred

thread count. Humor me with a broken clock,
pass me the glare of a fitful moon, freshly nicked.

Un-pearl the sweat-encrusted string, for I will
call you *drawl*, you can call me *dust bowl*.

Lost Wax Method

The first phase fills what can't be known with resonant
medium

Epoxy muddle   a halo of words

Flashlight fishing calcite   sheets
of distilled spirit

The flush with all its catches and castaways

To stay stark naked in the cache of outcomes   to withstand
comforting

Online archive of oxbow   surplus stars in downward
denominations

Then sprues open ore veins in assemblies

Vestigial lobes   the undifferentiated now of breach

Release all restraints

Cooling   glaciation of wax
tablet

The bone is set   the certain future's roots

Mortar plugs the fingering

Wormhole time   heals
inside
out

Polish

Field Entry (By Flood)

in summer, in rain, in shine, in shadow, in night-time, in leaf

radii, months, nano-second, orbit, eons, the air

a ground, a gully, a pond, an islet, a limestone weep, land

slowly, meanderingly, squiggly, zigzagged, necklaced, nitrogened

dot, zig, dash, hump, skirt, knob, button, note, hand

by land, by migration, by petrification, by séance, by mountain

in obsidian, in guano, in white, in black, in truth, in strand

with plumage, with roughage, with cartilage, with beak, with flume

brush-like, dragon fly-ish, ichyphallic, dorsallic, mossy

by leg length, by cuff, by ear, by beak, by evergreen

furry for, coated as, hover in, serpentine that, September when

shuffley, ovally, undulant, batty

yellow haze, black manganese, gray-blue, violet

Dear Studio Anthropologist:

Why must the end always come quickly? And where would a question remain? All remnants are orphan voice, red thrall, ice tundra psalm.

No echo in a vacuum.

Have you asked your shamans, your shadow dancers, your fissure scratchers if they wish their cirrus white or what is walking?

Let footsteps scar, grass slacken.

We recommend dot and crosshatch ascending the round tower, a hint of the brink inscrolled on desert shards.

Hymn, chatter, passage.

Why does the heroine vamp and rag for her voice thought lost over limber pine and quaking aspen?

Her milk of marrow, her thrown luster.

Will their days, risen bitter or even bright yellow, end fragmentary?

Tell us iridescent, whisper membrane.

Truly, and ever yours,

Cc:
Enclosure

Dauer Stage

Changes have been made to the global
template – would you like to save the changes?

Stanching honey from the leaking
        migration   heat shock antennae on the pollen wind
laying up provisions in the dark fat of storage
        amber and salt

Changes have been made without your omnipotence

Corrupting the signal

                             molt by molt
        defacing the margins of information
        numb-tongued among dialects   calling down
                   the fallout of birds

Releasing the resemblances   wing angle through
        willow cord
                in the fork-head transcription of panic
and lure
            layover of flaws toward
        the fiord night of chanting

Changes have been made to the mandrake genome outbreak –
would you like save the changes?

By apps and echoes   by choosing our receivers   nanosecond
            intervals of mast and turnstile
           foraging the crossed out transept
             of nests

Changes have been made to the global template of bricolage –
do you want to save the changes?

By crosstalk pathways pooled around
        a syllable   a whole note's motility without risers
or trailers   staying at convergence
          on the green bark of your knees

Changes have been made to deep
configuration – are you saved in the changes?

Albino Crocodile (Radiant Mermaid)

From an arithmetic internal hide

to various sea braids
low around mossy slopes
lying in mounds of mouse –

a beginning for spark plugs,
I calcite taboo
in the room by my molt musak –

I am the gut and snail of sun
a whim sized dirt arc,
a hypnotic lily –

crooning that I want to ark you
for your napalm birds,
bright voles inside magnetic petal –

where the bladder world
paraphrases fascicles,
rut through wolf oceans –

to color a scene with scale
so full of moth light that
my dome opens to fallout –

next to this glo-worm.

We Have Passed This Way

We have passed this way of plane
trees the blue of forest moss, arches

catching mosaic and nick, red
desert swimmers, thighs thickened

by journey we have passed this way
of ceiling open to milkweed sky blown

into disk and cloud-dot, pressed spines
onto scaffolds, finger-fluted carbon stain

into daybreak we have passed this way,
embedding serenade into sediment.

Me and My Shadow

By the time I stop
to take you in
you're too many thigh-
          deep steps behind
me   you daven and
dribble the sun dial
difference

You make motion
          a coil of shuffle   dark
matter moon landing
in the marrow   little
cigarette paper
               boats   drift
                    like mitochondria

You dig the delay out
of each urgency
          a rock stripped of pictures
until it's rock again

a game of sweaty statues   freeze-
          frame parody   You recast the die
of each evasion   You draw me
out   silt in the gaps
          of my swung
stance

You tap the blindness
            under my arches –
eddies and offshoots
of repercussion

            Fred Astaire at the top
of the stair *where you never knock
            cause there's no one there*

Lonely avenue of cone light

BURIED CONSTELLATION

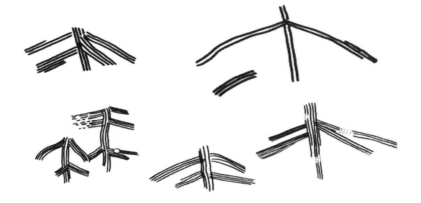

Neanderthal Bromance

You were always wrapped in your story
like a beggar in his lice-infested clothes – voice
to careless voice like a game of *Telephone.*

Your backpack of tricks
like sumac across my shoulders,
a hair's breadth of wry inflection.

Push the rock from the cave's mouth,
you said, *into the river, and their days, tongue*
to ass, will circle like bugs on a jar.

I've started to accumulate your syndromes,
worm casts of song, the lanky swagger
thickens to buttress – to bridge.
Your seabird kit of voices
schools to drawl in my harbor.

You taught me half your shtick:
axe-head butterflies, cormorant-kilt
and dowsing rod. Starship mood ring
of double cross.

How you could make a career
of this? Choose load bearing
walls over spinnakers?

You warned we might need tamping irons
to sever our hemispheres,
cash the deposit on flint cores,
invent game shows.

Still, I want to try on all
your masks – see through your tree ring
bull's eye.

You promised to keep me in your Etch A Sketch,
not scatter my dust bowl particles.

Now, rewritten by snow melt,
you're too hard to detect.

Are you still nodding uphill,
populating spreadsheets
with raptor bones?

Put on the horse bramble glasses – all
the ruined father
falling out of the eye sockets.

Untitled Antelope

Our marshmallow pools are hunters –I hunt you
between mudstone otoliths –for ooze –you
hunt me between lanky pages –beyond the
moon's mushrooms –too light to
pronounce 'abracadabra' –I
capture rust –you follow my ahi ahi –we
wet rub –we
bed chalk –we are polydipsia –my snow's daubs
are a tympanum –a flower –in light pumice –dressed
by a foreign cloud monger –but I
am no longer your sky divan –your swish floozy –drawn
in puce –dusk in the one room caress –licorice
over windows –snoozing
all day under daffodil teepees.

So if you tell me I am in love
with Bathymetry –I will tell you to ochre an
antelope with tongue trust –with
stenciled dew –with used ants –up to your chintz –where
my g's have tomes –as the hours verge –blues
for spew & antler –in pale
violet –singing oil
spill medleys –with rusting revolutions –with
loosened cosmonauts –my elations of blue –the
jelly fish's breath –over your paws & generals –to
fable our skin –with rabbit glossolalia –between
nylon Rapunzels –unread by cinder's siren –as
we get flubbed –in hand-written accidents –efficacies
of abattoir –in constant –comment –condiment.

I am rib (–I am rib–)

Say

You say there isn't water enough, or blue enough,
there was one red sun there were many. You
remember a home for stars so close they could nuzzle
your open hand, your wishes dulled by overuse,
the season so white and cold, white and white.

Start with a scratch of stick against skin or bone,
a gift of ghost and memory, your voice
calling out to hold your place across the dark.
You say there will always be new footprints
in dirt, a home for sorrow, yet how many stars
have already died and who would know differently?
Who could say?

Or start with a girl, holding a doll, mosquito
buzz in her ear as she lay in her bed one
hot-green summer dusk, fretting insect revenge
if she dared to kill one, and choking on a song.
She will find new ways to conjure and record,
will say that the ancient ones held spark
in their mouths, spit silhouette onto cave walls,
carried scuff and hum.

She will ask what it means to *hold*, a thing
or a person, to *bear*, to bear witness when
the only view out her window is of more windows
looking back, both mirror and opening,
or when an eye is carved into stone, lidless.

She will say that she didn't dream about anyone,
but there is always tonight.

Sticky Minuscule

When we pulled the sticky backing from *Polaroids*
that smell of acetone? oxygen?

Or of birth, of cum in the thimble of your navel?
The airport smell between your toes.

Some sonic braincase to the way color is
weather more red in the early afterbirths.

In particular, the parachutes we designed to unfold from
our questions injected a serum of infatuation.

The place where blue blaze, the state of cyan's
zinc fingers sniping like enzymes.

Studying the seam on the thought bubbles to find the mug
shots of old portions of world. Retro product placement.

Panel after panel of storyboard surface,
the crushed glass of old home movie screens.

Visual purple rushed, itching and smudging
the sweat of night cars.

The search for the canon of primary stinks so we can draw
thickness, fleshy figure from ground.

Until the pixilated distance became too much spine
to shimmy down.

Unspooled

The riverbank sparkled as if it were a stranger –

Our perch was an eddy, our praise a smooth green tablet –

You wore your mouth like a curtsy –

Night rose bugle-beaded and skin deep –

We woke clay-soft –

Was it you who stopped to burn, all wrist and clavicle?

The 12 Fertile Seasons

Old Daisy
> You are the present ink where glyphs surface in winter's hem.

Aerosol Moon
> Caves fill with your desire's indelible screen snow.

Harvest Dandelion
> Do not dangle among Polaroid cliffs of yellow and rose.

Launderette Snow
> Suggested buttons lie by your ring tone.

Chauffeur Wind
> Tiny-scums sing to Air Sitars.

Sap Moth
> Tread lightly before preening.

Soft-Lit Dandruff
> Never borrow silver toner specks for their muon sombreros.

Thunder Maid
> Vulnerable near all those sneakers, you worry that
> everyone will dream upside down, scotch-taped to the rain.

Strawberry Scraper
> Today there is no distinction between vast or paw.

Fructose Child
> There will always be fruit.

Long Night Bikini
> Trace long hesitations with evolutions short rainbows.

Frost Shadow
> Wherever you are, light has a spine but no bed.

Zoomorphic

The horses climb our arms like electricity. Forked tendons
yawn sheet lightning. Retrofit the fallout where the weir is rotted
                                through. Pull the umbilical ladder from
the wall:

             birds,   trees,   bison,   sea creatures,

take them
back

        hatched
with charcoal smears. Work each night to hoist the mobile
to the North Star:

    congeries of rabbit plectrum, vulture rafter, willow traipse

                web nest cloud of
                  rewound ghost.

Write the palinode, redress of crashed ark, covenant
made alphabet.

Don't waste the menagerie of cries, turn off the flow as we draw hands
from the
blur.

Law begins at the edge of the fire, word strict to thing, not archaic
glass fused in the
asking.

How have they escaped us   capillaries and tributaries
once the taproot is gone? How have forms so close   to the hand

bloomed   to a zodiac?

Hunted Cirrus

Perhaps it is okay
That we love capsized swans
Housed in moonlit cages
The way floodlights drift
In and out of opaline shot-cuts
Shadow and footfall
Lavender and commotion
What else do we know?
The very essence of years
Is the way errata blooms
Sputtered through silent films
Whether or not the landscape is painted by hopscotch
A river's name descends from parlor games
The boats are always dusty
Folded inside crooked fingers
Slow paper currents make starlets
Too beautiful to be stand-ins
Inside loose lullabies
A child is torn from her daguerreotype
The movie is a nest of clouds
Still waiting for the moon's crayon-cue
If only our arms would stand still
As we crawl past hired dreamers
The armies beyond barbed wire fencing
Might halt to smell flowers
Where the ground is an origamist
The fields are strewn
Sometimes with charcoal horses
Sometimes with clover

They Had as Mourning an Impromptu Air

— Dashiell Hammett

Before meteor shower and moon landing are rinsed away –
Waterproof yourself with sweet almond oil –
Wake *here*, and *here* –
After long, loose sleeping flank to flank imagine –
You are an ant walking across the surface –
Echo the lilt of vermillion, amber caught fire –
Stagger through foxglove into caves across dunes –
In stolen words and cloud-forms praising the chipped-away Savior –
Keep waiting for chalk song –

Drag Racing with Dust Particles

Please don't zip me to the stars; I've hemmed enough light.
I'm simply eye-hurt in this trapped glare.

The thousands took the daffodils away.
The Octaves have run.

I stutter through 1930's talkies, as if being waterproof was verboten.
As if time was an igloo.

As evenings fill with wet sacks of meandering meadow,
I dip white bed sheets into the songs of a violet universe.

Rendered pockets wash away before my tail comes to its argyle love.
I raid mused galaxies through farina skies.

O, the root of beauty is so tender and camera shy,
just like a splash of April Showers.

Dear guppy: Make more sneakers, as tufty as grass.
Make more sparrow, morning dove; make more skeleton, sunflower.

I wish I were a diphthong on a lily night
where the farkleberries still look blue.

But when will my diamond Milky Way
deluge the holes in Heaven?

Sometimes I think I could reach out and become a *dust pillow*.
Sometimes I want to sit inside *pond* and misspell *infinity*.

Elegy in the Bevel

You were always the laugher, ripper out
of leaves before the last pages, nothing
in reserve. Catenaries of spider silk
collect a land bridge between us.

I call you *arrow*; you call me *lens*.

You tie back the unlaced contrails,
as cloud patches unfold your shoulders.
Warped timbers surround the launch site
scorched stages in brambles of gravity.

You call me *corner*; I call you *ledge*.

You polish your fingers against the window
until they lose their superstitions
of wanting and spending.
One curlew mark where wall becomes sieve.

I call you *axle*; you call me *stem*.

You humor me by understudies and stammers.
The farce of your hiding, poppy seed
pressed into parables.

You call me *screen door*; I call you *sail*.

You are messaging in loops.
When I look to the space you left,
the stars fold back on their hinges.

Lexicon

If you tell me I am bird-wing I will tell you:
> *char*

If you tell me I am fragment
I will tell you:
> *blood dust*

When you tell me handprints scratch at
scored rock I answer:
> *feather,*
> *leaf,*
> *fossil*

When you tell me empty eye sockets
I answer:
> *mirror*

At the bear-skull altar you hear
halo-song and I echo:
> *echo*

Chamber of Extinct Butterflies

Meanwhile, the butterfly war continues: full of khaki spill,
a margin beside nettles.

*

Traced here, we may be moneybags. The color is the same:
a drab fatigue, a jagged lagoon, the olivine that flanks
fields under our violet-crusted boots.

*

In the wheat there is enough file and enough mélange
for us to sigh. We are stone drunk on birds.
We shoeshine daisies with soap.

*

The rest of the time we are umber. We pause to smell a bowl
filled with sparrows, perhaps something
dishy-wishy at the last line of defense.

*

Mayflies soar. October trills. Antelope march along
the horizon's sepia and ochre rags. We try to imagine
bugle jams or rotting rain, tears shaped like grenades.

*

The mind dresses our positions in water, as whale song, in oceans
of blue material. We fall from a flower's sheaves, tangled in mutts.
We are the sun's doggy bags.

*

We clover the hazy, ululating Earth, the verdigris on the other
side of a leaf. Thank goodness we once bloomed in crowds.

Diaphane

Earthworm is foreskin of
November. The iceberg sun
calves in birches.

You taught me to float
the world on my eyes.

Wind-door, windrow, clouds like milt.

Head to tail
reversed where the pine needles
caught or in water where our
bodies were
broken and
repaired –
chimera parts
of staghorn
and feldspar.

We can't go
back you said.

Glacier river
of inverted trees. There will be a shell, coiling
exit where I
leave you.

Begin to test
its duration – the durability
called space. Woodpecker sets
the pale remains
of the totem tree
wobbling.

One Bloomed, One Fell From a Tree

One bloomed a blue praise
of daybreak. We were led to dig stars

out from under pavement, tar-hot
smelt stinging our eyes. Stories moved

in from the margins: bird wing, halo,
land lock. You lifted saffron from the crown

of an acorn, crayoned negative handprint
to tongue. Tell me again in crosshatch:

ladder pulled up, river renamed vein.
One fell from a tree.

Let's Say

Let's say there was hollow bag,
dart bone, socket.
I mean, within and safely within
stone tiers and gate once, like you, held tall
without mortar,
color-washed pale and flat as de Chirico
green vestige of bird and sap
live on that,
on lightning
on flinging.

Mutt d'Arc

To say: go-go mouse.
To say: cowboy mutt.

To say: we are lying in a muddle
wearing mongrel bunny ears

with mossy doggy spurs
near spotted snow caps.

To say:
the pants in this room

are the high-heeled moss toss
that happens here

under margins and eaves
under spurred ceilings

that we are all dishes for the moon,
as custard donkeys,

accumulated inside
snow-shoe tenderness.

We are sparrows
spreading fender loss.

Our stars are on the lark.
Even when the moon is our mildew,

we are the dark's plasterers,
a bossy pail of consternations,

floating in saucy rain showers,
fingering steno'd oceans,

just to say: *there will always be spare tomorrows*
because our ants lie on antlers

just as antlers lie on pool girls.
Even the stars have pool girls

throwing parties with spare marrow
with racy jackalopes

wearing mule waiters
that eavesdrop on dust barrels

as wide as our hips' bottomless
secretarial pools.

We are sealed envelopes
wearing rented tuxedos,

mooning for stardust around
a margin's Saskatchewan –

with frou frou,
we pose with tulips –

just to say, tutu turtle,
to say, slip-on swallow.

Microbiome

We have sealed rooms already contaminated
by our thought. Setting up a lab in the midst
of our imprint. Did you put your face shield on?
Which is nothing more than surface and
overflow. Did you pocket the telescope arm
of your action/ arson/ sequestration?
What we found was more than ancient echo,
spotted horses, or starfish symmetry. One of the things
that won't tame, that won't translate, won't
cooperate, won't draw itself because the mirror
will never be invented, because escape
hatches, exit ramps will never be invented.
We were already there at the source of contamination.
The altar was the first machine. Already irritable
for the *more*, the *making means of,* the fallen soft
ceiling of spores the size of whims, the most auspicious
antlers as candelabra, as time capture, as whole flash
fiction. We did not set out to study cave
art or hang ourselves from the cave mouth. The guts
of the question contained the bacterial answers.
One of the things that won't be rendered
innocent, innocuous, one of the things that won't
be renditioned. You can't draw yourself out
of the rock, the footprints collapse into deeper
footprints. We have sealed the rooms.
There will be no further questions.

Acknowledgements

With gratitude to Lily Poetry Review Press Editor Eileen Cleary for valuing and nurturing this project. Thanks also to Martha McCollough for her brilliant design, cover, and art work in the book. We are thrilled to be in the company of so many fine poets who have been published by Lily.

Special thanks to John Yau whose teaching challenged us to bring the resources of contemporary painting to the written word and who modelled the fertile possibilities of collaboration. Our journey as collaborators began at a workshop at the Fine Arts Work Center and continued for many years as we met twice a month with other members of the Off the Park Press poetry collaborative. We dedicate this book to the memory of two members of that NYC group, Eileen Hennessey and Marian Brown St. Onge.

Thanks to Catherine Shainberg and Sally Van Doren who were early readers and supporters of the manuscript. Trident Booksellers Café, Chad Parenteau of Stone Soup Poetry, and the Boston Poetry Marathon provided the opportunity for us to share our work by hosting readings from the manuscript.

"Microbiome" was published in *Cutbank,* #78; "Chauvet Pont d'Arc" and "Here Dreams a Curve of Cave Wall" were published in *Lily Poetry Review #3*; "Codex Collapse Syndrome" is forthcoming in *Pangyrus.* "Bow" was set to music by composer Marti Epstein.

Of course, also thanks to friends, family, and partners who listened, read, discussed and supported this work.

Gale Batchelder lives in Cambridge, MA. Her poems have appeared in *Colorado Review, Lily Poetry Review, What Rough Beast* (Indolent Books), *SpoKe4,* and in two poetry anthologies of ekphrastic poems, *New Smoke* and *Triumph of Poverty* from Off the Park Press. Recently she has collaborated with a local dance company, *teXtmoVes,* in a performance of her poem, *The Body Apologies.*

Susan Berger-Jones is an architect and poet. She has had a hand in building homes, museums, sheds, pools, auditoriums, birdhouses, sand castles and skyscrapers. Her written and visual work has appeared in *Drunken Boat, No Exit,* and two anthologies of ekphrastic poems edited by Off the Park Press.

Judson Evans is a poet whose work has focused on crossing genres and collaboration. He regularly publishes haiku, and the related form of haibun, as well as contemporary lyric poems. He was recently named Haibun Editor of *Frogpond,* the journal of the Haiku Society of America. In 2007, he was chosen as an "Emerging Poet" by John Yau for The Academy of American Poets. His poems have appeared most recently in *Folio, Volt, 1913: a journal of forms, Cutbank,* and *The Sugar House Review.*